DATE DUE			
03/04/96			
SEP 26 1997			
MAR 10 1998			
MAY 07 1999			
DE 12 '00			
OC 15 '03			

TEEN HOT LINE

PREGNANCY

Cathie Cush

RSVP

RAINTREE
STECK VAUGHN
PUBLISHERS

The Steck-Vaughn Company

Austin, Texas

Consultants:
Jeanne E. Peranteau, Coordinator of Special Projects; Family Service Association of Bucks County, PA
Leni Zeiger Wildflower, Chair, Human Development Department; Harvard-Westlake School, Los Angeles, CA

Developed for Steck-Vaughn Company by Visual Education Corporation, Princeton, New Jersey
Project Director: Jewel Moulthrop
Editors: Dale Anderson, Paula McGuire
Editorial Assistant: Carol Ciaston
Photo Research: Cindy Cappa

Raintree Steck-Vaughn Publishers staff
Editor: Gina Kulch
Project Manager: Joyce Spicer
Electronic Production: Scott Melcer
Photo Editor: Margie Foster

Library of Congress Cataloging-in-Publication Data
Cush, Cathie, 1957-
     Pregnancy / Cathie Cush.
        p. cm—(Teen hot line)
     Includes bibliographical references and index.
     Summary: Covers a wide variety of topics related to teen pregnancy, including birth control, the question of abstinence versus sexual activity, peer pressure, precautions against disease, abusive partners, and life with a baby.
     ISBN 0-8114-3530-X
     1. Teenage mothers—United States—Juvenile literature. 2. Teenage pregnancy—United States—Juvenile literature. 3. Teenage parents—United States—Juvenile literature. 4. Sex instruction for teenagers—United States. (1. Pregnancy. 2. Teenage parents. 3. Sex instruction for youth.) I. Title. II. Series.
     HQ759.4.C87 1994
     306.7'0835—dc20   93-25155
                                                                          CIP   AC

Photo Credits: Cover: © Gabe Palmer/The Stock Market; **15:** Lloyd Wolf; **21:** © Tom Prettyman/PhotoEdit; **24:** © Blair Seitz/Photo Researchers; **34:** D&I MacDonald/Unicorn Stock Photos; **45:** Billy E. Barnes/PhotoEdit; **48:** Robert V. Eckert Jr./The Picture Cube; **49:** Polly Brown/The Picture Cube; **50:** Jeff Greenberg/Unicorn Stock Photos; **55:** Jeff Greenberg/Unicorn Stock Photos; **60:** Farley Andrews/The Picture Cube; **64:** © Gale Zucker/Stock Boston; **73:** © Rhoda Sidney/Stock Boston.

Printed and bound in the United States

1 2 3 4 5 6 7 8 9 0 LB 99 98 97 96 95 94 93

CONTENTS

What the

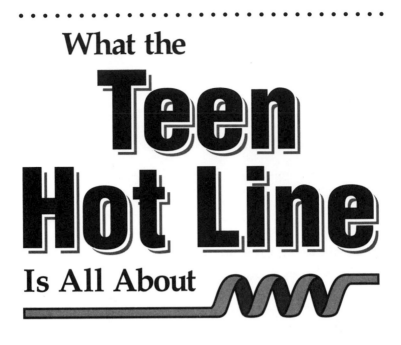

Teen
Hot Line

Is All About

This book is like a telephone hot line. It answers questions about teenage pregnancy that may bother you. In answering them, we will give you some important facts. You can use those facts to make your own decisions about sexual activity and pregnancy. So think of us as the voice on the phone, always there to answer your questions, even the ones that are hard to ask.

To help you think about how to approach this subject, here is a list of seven steps that we believe a person should take before deciding to have a sexual relationship. They focus on using common sense and finding out facts. They assume that you want to make your own decisions and that you want to behave responsibly both toward yourself and your partner.

Find out everything you can about human sexuality and birth control.

 Carefully consider the choice between abstinence and sexual activity. (Having sex with one partner doesn't mean that you are required to have sex with every partner that follows.)

 Talk to informed people to get the information you need, and talk frankly to your partner to communicate your decisions.

 Take precautions to avoid contracting or transmitting disease.

 Take precautions to avoid an unintended pregnancy.

 Examine your feelings and situation if pregnancy occurs and make an appropriate decision.

7 Avoid abusing your partner either physically or mentally.

After reading the book, we hope you will have some answers to your questions and perhaps to some questions you had not thought of yet. In the back of the book is a list of sources for further information. Thinking about the issues raised in this book is an important step toward taking control of your life.

Interview

Janet gave birth to twin girls—the result of an unplanned pregnancy—when she was 17. At the time of this interview, Janet did not think that she and the father of the twins would have a future together. Her goals were to finish high school, get a job at a hospital, and attend nursing school.

I'm 17, and I had identical twin girls about two months ago. One of them is home, and the other one is still in the hospital. She might be there for six months or a year.

I've been going out with the babies' father a little over a year. We're still together. I guess it's OK. Darryl helps with the baby. He lives about a five-minute walk away. He's going to be 20 next November.

I found out I was pregnant on June 3. I know exactly when I became pregnant, because we had been arguing that month and there was only one time we got together.

In school they tell you to use condoms. Darryl did that for a while, but I guess we got lazy about always using protection. Part of my problem is that I never paid attention in school. Besides, they tell you all this when you're a freshman. I was, like, so what? I wasn't going to do anything until I was married. I never did anything until I started going out with Darryl anyway.

Anyway, I didn't think about being pregnant. How I knew was, I get my period every 28 days. When I didn't get it, I waited 9 days without telling anybody. Nobody even knew I had sex. I'm 100 percent close with my sister. I told her on the ninth day. First I told her that I had sex, then I said I might be pregnant. The next morning we got a home pregnancy test, and it was positive.

The night before I took the test, I was making these deals with God. I said, "If I'm not pregnant, I'll never see Darryl again." I definitely didn't want to be pregnant. I saw at that time how serious it was.

If I wasn't pregnant, I wouldn't be with him now. Before I met him, I went out with a lot of guys. I knew what many guys wanted, but I would never let them have it. When I met Darryl, he was different. I never met anyone like him. He was at my house every minute of the day. He was 100 percent everything I wanted.

I was not really thinking about what I was doing when I was with him the first time. He wanted to get me pregnant. At my prom he told me, "I want a baby." I'm just brushing it off, thinking that he's just saying that; he's trying to trap me into staying with him. He knew me from before high school, and he knew that if a guy said something I didn't like, I'd just break up with him.

He knew I was late when it was five days. That night when I found out, we were arguing, you know, some dumb argument. Then when I told him, he said, "Oh, I love you; I'm going to stay with you." He was happy, but I sure wasn't. Now I had to try to make it work. And no matter what, I'll always have to stay in contact with him because of the girls.

Darryl didn't want me to have an abortion. It was like, "Don't even think about it." I never thought about not having the baby. I come from a religious family. I used to go to church two times a week. I always figured, if you can have sex, you have to deal with what could happen.

With adoption, I know I would never do it. I would never be able to live knowing I had a baby out there. And I have friends who've had abortions. Some have had three or four. It makes me sick. A lot of them were on birth control. It's an accident when it happens. They forget to take the pill one day, then keep having sex because they took it all the other days.

The reason I didn't get the birth control pill is, I went to a clinic and sat in the room where they showed you what everything was and how to use it. Then I set up an appointment to get birth control, but I couldn't get it for like a month and by that time I was pregnant.

When I told my mom I was pregnant, I thought she would flip out, but she was calm. I think she was just glad that I decided to go through with the pregnancy. When my brother was 16, he got a girl pregnant, but we didn't know it. Years later, we found out that he got her pregnant two times, and she had abortions both times. I guess my mom was glad because I could have had an abortion behind her back, but I didn't.

It was weird at school. It used to be, like, well, my friends were envious of me. But when I got pregnant, I felt like nobody looked up to me anymore. I felt insecure after I got pregnant. A lot of girls in my school were pregnant, but not once did I hang out with anybody else who was pregnant. I still have the same friends.

I found out I was having twins after five months . . . at my first ultrasound. I was shocked. I didn't believe the doctor when she told me. I was excited. Having twins was like crazy. I always wanted things to be different for me, and this was different. I wasn't scared. Why be scared? I figure, what's one more? Each step, I'm going to have to work a little harder. I'll have to feed two of them, and change one diaper, then the other, you know?

Everything with my whole entire pregnancy was unexpected—having to go in the hospital, the toxemia, the high blood pressure. I never was in the hospital overnight before. I went in to see my doctor, and she said, "You're already four centimeters dilated." She put me in the hospital, and they gave me some medicine to keep the babies inside me. I was there for two days, and I thought everything was OK. Then the next thing I know, they tell me in an hour they're taking them out. For seven days afterward, I was up in the ICU. I kept having high blood pressure.

When I had toxemia, I was close to having a heart attack or a stroke. I didn't know that until two weeks afterward. Then my one baby has this problem with her intestines, so she's still in the hospital. She might not be home for six months.

Taking care of the baby—at least just one for now—is easier than I thought. The hardest part is having to lug the baby around everywhere I go. It's like going on a mission.

The best part is she depends on me and nobody else. She needs me, and I guess I like to feel needed. I like thinking about seeing her through each stage through the rest of her life. I want to be there when she starts to walk and say her first word.

After I graduate, I want to go to nursing school. I might try to get a job at a hospital that would pay for nursing school.

As for Darryl and me, I don't really know what's gonna happen. When I was pregnant, I was limited to where I could go, and he wasn't around that much. Now I can do what I want, go places I want. Now he's more attached. I'm more my old self, so he feels more attached. If I met somebody else, I would break up with him and forget about him, but for now I'm holding on.

If I have to go to work and miss being there for their first steps, I'd be mad. I don't want to miss out on them. Teenagers, they think it's fine and dandy to have a baby with a person you love. They don't realize you're dealing with insurance and paperwork the rest of your life. It's not all it's cracked up to be.

My main lesson was with Darryl. I guess I would say, think about what you're doing before you do it. You can't turn back. Think about what kind of future you would have with this person. I didn't think about all the days we were arguing. I think we'll stay together for a while, but not forever. I don't need him anymore. Darryl made me feel needed when I was pregnant. Now the babies make me feel needed.

BULLETIN BOARD

Sexual Activity

Percent of females who have had sexual intercourse by age 15: 27

Percent of females who have had sexual intercourse by age 19: 78

Percent of males who have had sexual intercourse by age 15: 33

Percent of males who have had sexual intercourse by age 19: 86

Average age of first intercourse: 16

Sexually Transmitted Disease

Estimated number of HIV-positive people between the ages of 13 and 24: 78,000

Number of teens who contract gonorrhea in a year: 200,000

Number of reported cases of chlamydia in the U.S. in 1991: 362,000

Teenage Pregnancy

Developed country with the highest rate of teen pregnancy: United States

Approximate number of American teenagers who become pregnant per year: 1 million

Percent of pregnancies that are unplanned: 85

Percent of sexually active females who become pregnant by age 18: 25

Percent of teen mothers who have a second pregnancy within two years: 31

State with the highest teen pregnancy rate: California

State with the lowest teen pregnancy rate: Wisconsin

Contraceptive Use

Percent of teens who use contraception regularly: 20-30

Percent of males 15-19 who use condoms: 57

Most common reasons for not using contraception:

- 41% thought it was the wrong time of the month to become pregnant
- 9% were pregnant or trying to become pregnant

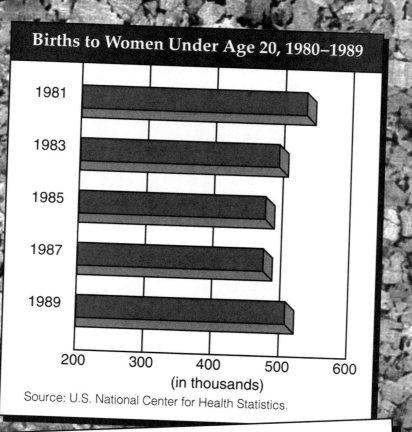

Births to Women Under Age 20, 1980–1989

	(in thousands)
1981	
1983	
1985	
1987	
1989	

200 300 400 500 600
(in thousands)

Source: U.S. National Center for Health Statistics.

Approximately one million teenage girls become pregnant each year; and about 50 percent of teenage pregnancies end in births.

Sources: The Alan Guttmacher Institute.

Centers for Disease Control, National Center for Prevention Services.

Planned Parenthood Association.

Communicating

 Q What should I do? My name is Beth. I'm 16. I'm worried and confused about things. I've been going with Bobby for a couple of months now, and I really like him a lot. I know he wants to have sex, but I'm not sure I'm ready. And I'm afraid to bring it up.

A Yes, it's difficult to talk about sex with your boyfriend. But talking now may save a lot of grief later. Is it the right time to become sexually active? Do you know how to protect yourself from becoming pregnant or from getting sexually transmitted diseases? The decisions you make about sex could affect the rest of your life—you owe it to yourself to make them carefully. Maybe you should talk them through with a close friend first, or even with one of your parents.

• • • • • • • • • • • •

 Q Talk to my parents about sex? Are you kidding?

A No, not at all. Of course it may be difficult for you. You're sure they'll be too disapproving even to talk generally about sex, and you may be right. But remember this: they were young once, and they care about you. They could give you some advice and information.

However, it's your decision. You might prefer to borrow from the experience of another adult you feel close to—a counselor or minister, an aunt or uncle, a friend's parent, or an older brother or sister. You could talk to a friend your own age, though such a person is likely to have less knowledge. You could explore some of these issues by reading a book. But you owe it to yourself to find out everything you can. Examine the pros and cons of becoming sexually active, find out the risks involved in having sex, and then make a decision.

• • • • • • • • • • •

Q Well, I just don't see talking to my parents, or any adult about this. I'd talk to Bobby before them.

A You should talk to Bobby. Even though it may not be easy to do so, it's very important. And don't wait until the last minute—when there's a danger of things getting out of control. He must know how you feel, not just about him, but about having sex. Of course, you're nervous about talking to him because you don't know how he'll react. But having sex is an important decision in your life, and he must understand what it means to you.

You say you're afraid to bring up the subject with Bobby. That's understandable, especially because you're not sure how you feel. You're worried and confused and don't want to think about birth control just now. Maybe you have a moral objection to sex before marriage. Maybe you think you should be committed to your partner first. Maybe—as much as you like Bobby—you aren't ready to become sexually active. A lot of 16-year-olds aren't. There's no rule that says you have to. Better to postpone having sex if you aren't sure.

• • • • • • • • • • •

What if he doesn't like me anymore?

It's true, many girls do worry that boys will be turned off if they express any doubts or fears about having sex. There's sure to be some embarrassment, maybe some resistance. Bobby may insist. He may not show much concern at first for your feelings. Even if he's pleased that you've brought up the subject, it may be hard for him to respond easily.

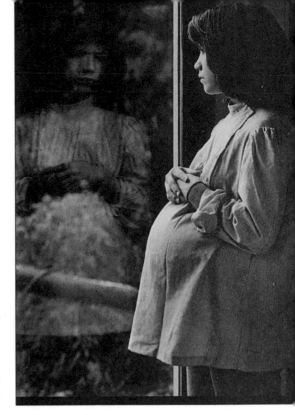

Having a baby makes an enormous difference in a teenager's life.

It will be easier for you to talk if you do some advance planning. Here are some suggestions on how to make your decision and then how to talk about it.

Making Your Decision

A good way to start is to get your thoughts together. Know exactly what you want to say.

■ Examine the facts. Learn as much as you can about human sexuality and the possible consequences of having sexual intercourse. You already know that having sex is more than being caught up in a romantic moment. Understand the risks of becoming pregnant. Know the risks of contracting sexually transmitted diseases, including AIDS. What you learn now could save your life!

■ Examine your feelings. Know exactly how you feel about becoming sexually active. Think through why you are worried and confused. How do you feel about Bobby? How do you think he feels about you? If necessary for your well-being, are you willing to lose him? Try to think of ways events might turn out and how you might feel about them before making a decision.

■ Make your decision.

Learning How to Communicate

There are things you can do to get over the hurdles of communicating your decision.

■ Know what you want from the conversation. Are you looking for help in making up your mind or do you want to explain your feelings?

■ Plan in advance what you are going to say and how you will say it.

■ Decide when you are going to bring up the subject. It is best to talk at some quiet moment, when you are both relaxed and at ease. Be prepared to seize the moment when it appears; you may not know exactly when it will happen. Telling your partner what you feel before you get close is important. But even if you are in the heat of the moment, you can still say "No!"

Opening the Conversation

Let's say, after thinking it all over, you've decided against having sex. How will you bring the subject up without hurting

Bobby's feelings? Here are some suggestions. Choose one or make up your own.

"I need to talk to you about something important—for both of us."

Or, "Something is happening between us that I think we need to talk about."

Or, "This is going to be hard for me to say, but I really care about you and have to say it."

Having the Conversation

Once you've started, the hardest part is over. You have already planned that you'll say something like the following:

"Bobby, you know how much I like you, but I feel things are going too fast for me. I've decided I'm not ready to have sex with you and I want to talk about it."

Let Bobby know exactly how you feel. Then give him a chance to respond. Really listen to what he says. He'll need to talk about his feelings, too. Look at him while he's talking. Tell him when you agree with him. Don't argue. And don't let him think you blame him. Reassure him that you care about him.

Maybe he'll say, "How come you let me fool around so much, then? That's not fair."

Or, "But, I love you. And I want to be with you. Everybody else is doing it. There's nothing wrong with it."

Or, "Actually, I'm a little confused myself. I thought maybe you didn't want to, and I'm glad you told me."

A variety of feelings may be expressed in this conversation— fear, anger, rejection, love, relief, a new sense of closeness. Be prepared to talk about things he wants to talk about and explain your position clearly. If he agrees with you, fine. But if he is very angry and insistent, you may have to take a stand. In this case it will be important for you to make it clear that you have made a decision and intend to stick by it. You may even have to walk away from the conversation for the moment.

Don't try to go too fast. One conversation may not be enough. You both may need to talk more at another time to clear up all the feelings. Keep the communication channels open. Let him know you're willing to discuss the situation.

And remember. Decisions about sex are not permanent. Just because you've decided for now not to have a sexual relationship doesn't mean you never will. What is important is that you feel comfortable with your decision.

Sticking to Your Decision

Once you've made your decision and talked with Bobby, there are some situations you need to be prepared for.

■ Don't be talked out of your decision. You can change your mind, but only when you decide to do so.

■ Don't send Bobby mixed messages. Be consistent. If you act in a sexy way, he may be confused about what you really mean.

■ Don't put yourself in situations that might make it hard for you to stick to your decision. Try not to spend all your time with him alone. Get together with friends and go to sports activities or to the movies.

■ Drugs and alcohol could make it hard for you to stick to your decision. They affect your judgment, your inhibitions, and your behavior. Don't put yourself in the position of wondering, "What happened last night?"

No matter what your decision is about having sex, making that decision by yourself is a major accomplishment. Deciding on your own is the difference between being a kid and becoming an adult. Learning how to think through a situation rationally as well as emotionally is sometimes difficult and painful. But, once learned, it is a skill you will use for the rest of your life.

CHAPTER 2

Avoiding Pregnancy

 My girlfriend wants me to wear a condom. Can't she just go on the pill?

A Maybe she can go on the pill. Her doctor or a family planning center can best determine that. But you are both responsible for preventing pregnancy and the spread of diseases. And condoms are essential. Short of abstinence, latex condoms, or rubbers, are the best way to reduce the spread of sexually transmitted diseases (STDs), including AIDS. Each method of birth control has its own advantages and disadvantages. Both of you need to find out what is available, then decide together which method or methods you want to use.

• • • • • • • • • • • •

Protection from pregnancy and diseases should be uppermost in your mind when you make the decision to have intercourse. Here is some information that might help you make your choices.

Fertilization

About once a month, one of a woman's two ovaries releases a ripe egg, which travels down the fallopian tubes toward the uterus. Most of the time, the egg breaks apart and the woman has her period as usual.

Pregnancy occurs when a male sperm fertilizes the egg, usually after intercourse, and the fertilized egg attaches itself to the spongy lining of the uterus. Sometimes penetration doesn't even have to take place. If a male ejaculates on the lips of a female's vagina, some of the sperm might reach the egg anyway. The sperm release special enzymes that dissolve the egg's outer layer. One sperm is drawn into the egg and fertilization occurs. It takes only one sperm to fertilize an egg for a female to become pregnant, and males release as many as 400 million sperm when they ejaculate.

Many contraceptives work by blocking the sperm from reaching the egg or by killing them before they can fertilize it. Others use artificial hormones (chemicals that produce a specific response) to prevent the ovaries from releasing an egg. There are also contraceptive methods based on not having sex or using extra protection when a woman is most fertile.

The only method of birth control that's 100 percent effective in preventing pregnancy (and the spread of STDs) is not having sex at all.

The possibility of an unwanted pregnancy or STD is only one reason not to have sex. For most people, sex is an emotionally intense experience, and you might not feel you are ready for it. You might not feel especially close to the person who wants to have sex with you. You might not have other birth control available at a particular time. Or you just don't feel like doing it.

Danielle, 15, was a virgin when she started dating Sean, 16, three months ago. She still is.

"A little while ago, Sean started saying that we should have sex," Danielle said. "I really like Sean a lot, but I'm not sure how I feel about sleeping with somebody now. I might feel different if we're still together six months from now."

Danielle talked with Sean about her mixed feelings. They decided that having sex at this point would put too much pressure on their relationship. They decided to wait.

"Ever since then, we've been getting even closer emotionally. I really respect Danielle for sticking to her beliefs," Sean said.

There are various ways to be caring and loving with your partner without having sex. You'll be surprised how the most ordinary activity can become special for you both. You might:

make the other person feel important and respected

hold hands

talk on the phone

hide a love note where the other person will find it

share a secret

use eye contact to share a private thought

give or get a hug

make plans for your future

Contraceptives

If you decide at any point in any relationship to have sex, you will want to use protection. There are a number of options that are available to you and your partner.

Two people can show their affection for each other without having sex.

Condoms

Condoms are latex or animal skin sheaths that fit over the penis when it is erect and catch sperm when a man ejaculates. Rubbers, as condoms are also called, are inexpensive (about 50 cents each), and you can get them at drugstores without a prescription. They're even sold in vending machines in many locations. You use them only when you're having sex, and they have no side effects.

Latex condoms are the best way to protect yourself and your partner from diseases such as chlamydia, gonorrhea, herpes, and AIDS. Latex condoms are better at preventing disease than the animal skin types.

Some guys don't like to use condoms. They think rubbers aren't "macho" or that the sheath will reduce their sexual pleasure. That's an irresponsible way of thinking. Guys need to share responsibility for preventing pregnancy and disease—for their own sake, as well as for their partner's. The condom won't really interfere with a guy's sensations, and both partners will be free of the worry about pregnancy and disease.

Marilena, 18, insists that her partners use condoms. "I didn't always. When I was younger, I used to believe it when guys told me that birth control is the girl's responsibility, because she's the one who gets pregnant," Marilena said. "Now I see that's stupid. One of my friends got herpes because she used a diaphragm, and her boyfriend wouldn't wear a rubber."

When using a condom, it's important to put it on before the penis gets near the vagina, and to make sure it doesn't slip off when the guy withdraws. Condoms come prelubricated (coated with a moistening substance) or not. If a lubricant is needed, use water-based lubricants only. Oil-based lubricants, like petroleum jelly, can be irritating and can cause holes in the condom. A condom should be used only once, then thrown away.

When used correctly, condoms are about 98 percent effective in preventing pregnancy and diseases. They're even more effective if used in combination with a contraceptive foam.

Spermicides

Vaginal foam, cream, and jelly are different kinds of spermicides—chemicals that kill sperm. Used alone, spermicides are about 70 to 85 percent effective, but they are more than 98 percent effective if condoms are also used. Some foams, jellies, and condom lubricants contain an ingredient called nonoxynol-9, which may even offer some protection against STDs.

Like condoms, spermicides can be purchased at a drugstore without a prescription. They are small and easy to carry, so you can always have them available.

If there is any drawback to spermicides, it's that you have to remember to insert them into the vagina no more than 20 minutes before sex. Some people might think of using foam or putting on a condom as a bothersome interruption, but either step is an important precaution. Taking a few minutes to use birth control is easier than dealing with an unwanted pregnancy, the effects of which can last for a lifetime. Sometimes spermicides can be messy or drippy, but they also help lubricate the vagina. A few people may be allergic to the spermicide or to a particular brand. They need to try different brands or switch to a different form of protection.

Diaphragm

A diaphragm is a small rubber cap that fits inside the vagina over the cervix, the opening to the uterus. It blocks sperm from entering the uterus, preventing fertilization. It must be used with a spermicidal jelly or cream and can be put in place up to two hours before sex. A diaphragm has an effectiveness rate of about 97 percent when used correctly.

A diaphragm must be specially fitted to each woman's shape by a doctor or other clinician, and it takes some practice to learn how to insert and remove it properly. Most women don't feel the diaphragm at all once it is in place.

Leave the diaphragm in place for six or eight hours after having sex. After it's removed, follow the manufacturer's directions, wash it with warm, soapy water, and store it in its container. Before using it again, hold it up to the light and check for holes or tears. With care a diaphragm can last two years.

Sponges

Similar to diaphragms, contraceptive sponges keep sperm from reaching the uterus. These small, disposable sponges fit

A trained pharmacist can also give advice about which birth control method is the best one to use.

over the cervix and contain spermicides that are released over a 24-hour period. They can be put in place several hours before having sex, so there are no interruptions, and they can be left in place if you're going to have sex more than once within a 24-hour period. The sponge must be left in for at least 6 hours following intercourse. Then you throw it away.

You can buy sponges in the drugstore for about $1.50 each. Sponges come in sterile, sealed packages about the size of a golf ball, and they fit easily into a purse.

Sponges alone aren't quite as effective as a diaphragm. They can't be used during menstruation, because they could contribute to a condition called toxic shock syndrome, a serious illness caused by bacteria. They may increase the chances of vaginitis and can make intercourse dry. If that happens, use a water-based lubricant.

The Pill

Next to not having sex at all, probably the most effective method of birth control is the birth control pill. The pill uses a combination of artificial hormones to prevent the monthly release of an egg. No egg, no fertilization, no pregnancy. Pretty simple. However, the pill offers no protection against STDs, including AIDS.

A clinician must prescribe the pill, and it must be taken exactly as prescribed. By establishing a routine and taking the pill at the same time every day, it's less likely to be forgotten. It's easy to use, and it won't interfere at all with lovemaking.

Not everyone can take the pill, although most young women can if they're in good health and don't smoke. At first, it might cause weight gain, moodiness, or spotting between periods, but these symptoms usually go away after two or three months. If not, talk to a doctor or clinician at a family planning clinic. The pill can also have some serious side effects, such as high blood pressure, so it's necessary to get a physical, including a pelvic examination, at least once a year if you're taking it.

Donna's medical history showed that her mother took medication for high blood pressure. Donna's blood pressure was normal, but since the tendency for high blood pressure can be inherited, her doctor didn't want to take any chances.

"For the first year I was on the pill, she made me come back for a blood pressure check every three months. She said if my blood pressure went up, I'd have to switch to another kind of birth control," Donna related.

Norplant™

Women who like the idea of the pill, but who don't want to remember to take it every day, may prefer a relatively new contraceptive called Norplant™. With Norplant, tiny capsules containing artificial hormones are inserted under the skin of the arm. The hormones are released slowly into the bloodstream for up to five years. It's more than 99 percent effective, because there's nothing to forget, nothing to break, nothing to slip out of place.

For young people, the biggest drawback to Norplant is cost. Although it probably costs about the same as the pill over a five-year period, you need to pay for Norplant's protection up front. Also, minor surgery is necessary to implant or remove the capsules.

Natural Family Planning

You may have religious or moral reasons for not using contraceptives, but you still want to have sex without having a baby. Natural family planning is based on not having sex during the most fertile time of a woman's menstrual cycle. This method is not always as reliable as other forms of birth control, but it can be effective, it costs nothing, and has no side effects.

Natural family planning does take some effort. Users must take classes to learn the changes in body temperature, vaginal mucus, and other signs that signal fertility. Then they must be willing to chart these conditions every day.

Using Birth Control

The key to effective birth control is using whatever method or methods you choose correctly each time you have sex. This is difficult if you're using drugs or alcohol, which can weaken both your judgment and your willpower. It's also difficult if one partner is unhappy about the choice of contraceptives. That's why it's important for both of you to make the decision about what method to use.

Myths and Misconceptions

■ *Pregnancy won't occur if the male withdraws before ejaculation.* Before a male ejaculates, sperm in the seminal fluid can reach the female's uterus.

■ *Birth control is the female's responsibility.* It takes two partners to have sex and for fertilization to occur. A pregnancy will affect the lives of both partners, so both partners need to take responsibility for birth control.

■ *If a male doesn't ejaculate, he can hurt himself.* A male can't do any damage to himself by getting aroused and then not having sex, although this myth is common among young people. When a male gets excited, one of the things that happens is increased blood flow to the genitals. If he doesn't have an orgasm, he may be left with an uncomfortable feeling of fullness or tightness for a while, but this goes away.

■ *Birth control isn't necessary if a girl is a virgin or if she has her period.* Many females have become pregnant the very first time they had sex. You should use birth control every single time. Depending on when she ovulates, or releases an egg, a female may be able to get pregnant if she has sex during her period. It's best not to take chances.

■ *Stopping to use birth control takes the spontaneity out of having sex.* Some methods of birth control, like the pill, are "invisible." They don't involve stopping to do anything. Using condoms, foam, or a diaphragm can be made part of having sex. And they're much easier to deal with than a pregnancy or sexually transmitted disease.

If you have more questions about preventing pregnancy and STDs, see the resources listed in the back of this book, or talk to your parents, your doctor, or a counselor at a family planning center.

If You Think You're Pregnant

Q I should have had my period last week. Do you think I could be pregnant? How can I tell for sure? Maybe I'm worried for no reason.

A Maybe you are worried, and the stress has made your period late. Then again, if you've had sex in the past month, a missed menstrual period is a very strong sign that you could be pregnant. Wouldn't you rather know for sure? If you miss a period, you should get a blood or urine test as soon as possible to determine if you are pregnant. If you don't want your parents to know yet, or can't confide in your family doctor, you can be tested at a local clinic, such as Planned Parenthood. If you find out that you are pregnant, you'll need time to make some very important decisions. If you find out that you're not pregnant, it will take a lot off your mind. A home pregnancy test will not be effective until two weeks after your missed period. But you can get a blood test at a clinic as soon as you think you are late.

• • • • • • • • • • • •

The possibility of pregnancy is a reality for any sexually active couple, even if they are using birth control. Remember, abstinence is the only 100 percent sure way to avoid pregnancy. Anytime a male ejaculates in or even on the lips of a female's vagina, pregnancy is a possible outcome. Let's talk about what you may be facing.

Signs of Pregnancy

A missed period is the most obvious sign of pregnancy. However, it might also be a sign of sickness, stress, or the irregularity that many teenage girls experience. On the other hand, a female could be pregnant and still have a period, although it will probably be shorter than usual. Other signs to look for might include breast tenderness and darkening of the colored part of the nipples; the need to urinate more frequently than usual; a feeling of nausea in the morning, evening, or all the time; fatigue or dizziness; and weight gain. But in most cases, a missed period will be the most obvious clue.

If you have had sex recently and you experience one or more of the above signs, you should arrange for a pregnancy test as soon as possible.

Denial

Some women who are facing an unplanned pregnancy put off taking a pregnancy test. Some do it for financial reasons. They're afraid that the test will cost too much. It's important to know that most health clinics will charge only as much as a client can afford to pay.

Other women won't take a test because they don't want to believe or accept the fact that they might be pregnant. Ignoring the issue won't make it disappear. Neither will wishing, douching, soaking in a hot bathtub, or falling down the stairs. Believe it or not, women who didn't want to be pregnant have tried all these things. They just don't work, and they could harm the mother.

Tanya's period was a few days late. But because she wasn't always regular, she didn't do anything about it, even though she had had unprotected sex with her boyfriend once in a while. She waited until she had missed a second period to get a pregnancy test. By then she was almost two months pregnant. The safest abortions are those done within the first three months of pregnancy. That didn't leave her much time to make up her mind. Tanya had an abortion, but she later felt that she might have chosen differently if she hadn't been under pressure to decide so quickly.

Regardless of whether you decide to keep the baby or terminate the pregnancy, it's best to know if you're pregnant as early as possible. The sooner you know for sure that you're pregnant, the more time you will have to make important decisions regarding your pregnancy and the better care you can take of yourself. If you put off taking the test, and it turns out that you are pregnant, you may limit your options and deprive yourself and the baby of important early prenatal (before birth) care. Finding out early is better for everyone involved.

Pregnancy Tests

Pregnancy tests detect HCG, a hormone that a pregnant female's body produces when the fertilized egg implants itself in her uterus. HCG can be detected in the urine or blood.

Urine tests contain a chemical that reacts, usually by changing color, when it detects HCG in the urine. The test is relatively inexpensive and can be administered by a doctor, a hospital, a clinic, or a pregnancy lab. Home versions of the same test also are available at many drugstores.

A urine test is not effective until two weeks after the start date of the missed period. If the test reacts, you are pregnant. If the test does not react, you may not be pregnant—or it might be just too soon to tell. HCG levels might not be high enough yet for the test to detect them. False negative readings are not uncommon, especially with the at-home tests. If a urine test reads negative and you still don't get your period, have another test done by a health care professional.

A blood test can detect pregnancy about 10 to 14 days after conception, because it's more sensitive than a urine test. A blood test, however, is usually more expensive, and the blood sample must be taken by a health care professional.

A positive test should be followed by a pelvic examination. By looking for changes in the cervix and uterus, a doctor will be able to confirm pregnancy. He or she can also recommend a prenatal care program to help keep both mother and baby healthy.

Prenatal Care

During pregnancy, nearly everything the mother does affects the developing baby. (The baby is called an embryo during the first eight weeks of development, and a fetus from the ninth week until birth.) Anything the mother eats, drinks, or smokes reaches the baby. This is true throughout the pregnancy, but it is especially critical during the first three months, or first trimester, when the baby is developing most rapidly. Alcohol, caffeine, cigarettes, or drugs—even aspirin and cold remedies—can harm the baby. They can cause low birth weight, retarded development, deformities, or brain damage. In fact, women who are planning a family should stop using these substances before they get pregnant.

Pregnancy places various demands on the mother's body, so it's important to get enough nutrients for both mother and baby. Young teenage mothers-to-be should take particularly good care of themselves, because pregnancy is often more physically stressful for them than it is for women in their 20s. Good nutrition is critical, and exercise can help keep the body strong.

An obstetrician, a doctor who specializes in treating pregnant women, can make recommendations about diet, nutritional supplements, exercise, and appropriate weight gain. At regular visits, he or she will also monitor fetal development to make sure that the pregnancy is progressing as it should.

Making Decisions

Don't be surprised if you experience many different emotions after you find out for sure that you are pregnant. Even if you don't want to be pregnant, you might feel glad that you are. You may be proud, depressed, excited, angry, happy, scared, or relieved. You may feel some or all of those emotions to differ-

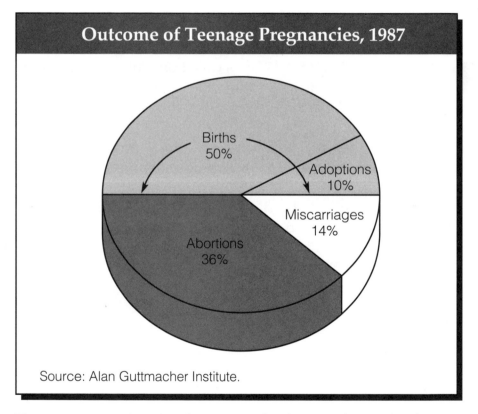

Outcome of Teenage Pregnancies, 1987

Births 50%

Adoptions 10%

Miscarriages 14%

Abortions 36%

Source: Alan Guttmacher Institute.

The reasons most often given by teenagers for choosing abortion or adoption are: concern about the changes a baby will make in their lives, feeling that they are not mature enough to be a parent, concern about not having enough money to raise a child.

ent degrees at different times—and that's perfectly normal. You may not feel at all the way you expected to feel.

The important thing is, now that you know, you are faced with one of the most important decisions of your life. You must choose whether to keep the baby, have the baby and give him or her up for adoption, or terminate the pregnancy. Many people can help you deal with your feelings and make your choice, but ultimately it is your decision. No one can make it for you, and no one has the right to force you to do anything against your will.

Get as much good, solid information as you can on your options. You'll also need to explore your feelings. You may want to talk to the baby's father, your own parents, and/or a trusted counselor. They can help you clarify your feelings and your values, and they can provide a support network for you once you've made your decision.

The most important question you need to ask yourself is this: *Am I ready to raise a child at this point in my life?* Be very honest when you answer. You'll live with your decision the rest of your life. Here are some other questions to ask:

Am I mature enough to be responsible for a baby that depends on me completely?

How will having a baby affect my future goals? Will I be able to finish school? Will I have to give up plans for college?

Can I afford to support myself and a baby? Will my parents help? Will the baby's father help?

Do I have strong religious or moral values that I would go against if I choose to have an abortion?

Am I acting out of fear and choosing an abortion just so I won't have to tell my parents I'm pregnant?

Do I want to keep the baby just so the father will marry me? What if he changes his mind later?

Many teens have been involved in unplanned pregnancies. A school guidance counselor is a source of valuable information at such a stressful time.

■ Am I willing to give up my free time with my friends to take care of a baby that needs to be fed, changed, cuddled, doctored, and constantly watched?

You're the only one who can answer these and the many other questions facing you when you learn that you are pregnant. But talking to others is usually helpful, too. People who care about you can help you sort out your feelings and offer insights that you may not have alone. There is no one right answer—only an answer that is right for you.

The Father's Role

It may sound obvious, but a girl doesn't get pregnant by herself. Usually, the focus is on the girl, but the guy is involved, too. Often the guy feels left out—or actually gets left out—of the process once he has contributed his sperm.

Some girls tell their boyfriends when they first think they're pregnant. Some guys are willing to help pay for the pregnancy test or go with the girl to the doctor's office or the clinic. At any rate, now they need to make a decision that will affect both their lives.

The girl should talk to the baby's father about her feelings and find out what he feels. Chances are, he'll want to support her in whatever decision she makes. And he'll need her support, too. Even though the mother is the one who carries the baby, the father is probably experiencing a lot of the same confusing emotions she is: pride, anger, relief, anxiety. You can help each other deal with your feelings.

The two of you may have been planning to get married someday, or maybe you are willing to make that commitment to each other now. Or maybe you'll decide to keep the baby without getting married, and you'll share financial responsibility for the child. Or maybe you'll both decide that an abortion is the answer. Both of you will need to discuss the questions above. Don't be afraid to get into details: where will you live, how will you pay for things, what kind of job can you find?

Maybe the guy won't be understanding. For example, the thought of being a father was so scary to James that he denied being the father of Lisa's baby, even though he knew he was her only boyfriend. He got very angry and accused Lisa of having sex with someone else. They broke up and went their separate ways. After the baby was born, Lisa sued James for child support. The judge made him take a blood test, and the results proved that James fathered the baby. James had to pay financial support until the child turned 18, even though he wasn't involved with Lisa any longer.

Facing the Folks

You've just accepted the news of a pregnancy when you suddenly realize you have to tell your parents, too. For some teens, this is almost the worst part. Lots of kids fear their parents' reactions. It's true that your parents might be hurt or shocked or angry at first. Believe it or not, they're probably just as frightened and worried as you are. But once most parents deal with their own feelings, they can be very understanding and helpful. Most parents do care very much about their children. And they're concerned about how an unplanned pregnancy will affect the future of their child.

Besides, although it's not easy for some kids to accept it, all parents were teenagers once themselves. Many parents recall their own feelings as teenagers when dealing with their kids' problems. They also know from experience that parenthood is a long, difficult task. Your parents have a lot of wisdom to offer. Their understanding and support can be very valuable while you're trying to make up your mind about how to handle the pregnancy.

However, some parents just cannot accept the fact that their unmarried child is involved in a pregnancy. They may be against sex before marriage for religious reasons. They might have different ideas from you about what is right or wrong. In some cases, parents receiving this kind of news react in extreme ways, justifying their child's fears. Family counseling might be very helpful in such a case.

You're the one who has to decide whether your parents will be able to adjust to the idea of a pregnancy. If you already communicate with them frankly, they will probably be receptive to discussing even the subject of pregnancy. If you don't already talk with your parents about a lot of things, it may be difficult to bring up the subject. Whether or not you think they will support you, make every effort to tell them. You might be surprised by their reaction.

Other Sources of Support

Ideally, you will be able to talk to your parents about the pregnancy. But, if talking to your parents doesn't seem like an option, or if you want an adult point of view from someone you feel will be more objective, you have many resources.

The health care provider who performed the pregnancy test and/or pelvic exam may be able to direct you or your partner to a counselor or social worker who is experienced with teen pregnancies. Most hospitals have social service departments that can help you. Counselors on staff at family planning or birth control clinics have helped countless young men and women sort out their feelings about an unplanned pregnancy. Health care providers are a good source of information on the medical matters involved in a pregnancy as well as the social and emotional ones. Whether you decide to look for an obstetrician or an adoption agency, or get an abortion, a health care provider can probably give you a list of local contacts.

A guidance counselor at your school can also provide you with valuable information. He or she is trained specifically to handle teenagers' problems and will keep anything you say confidential.

The important thing to remember is that there is help available, no matter how alone you might feel. Many other teens have been involved in unplanned pregnancies. Be comforted with the knowledge that others have had many of the same confused feelings you have. And they have had to work through the same questions and make as important a decision about the future as you will. Above all, let people help you. Support from people you trust can make it easier to come to a decision with which you can feel comfortable.

Interview

Darryl is 19 years old and the father of Janet's twins. He is a high school graduate and is currently working as a laborer. Darryl tried as much as possible to help Janet through a difficult pregnancy. As he stated in this interview, he remains concerned about Janet and their babies.

I guess I found out in June that Janet was pregnant. I was happy because it was part of me, something that was mine and hers coming into the world. But I was scared because of all the pressures that come along with it.

I didn't want to think about the stuff that made me scared. I was really concerned about Janet and how she was going to take it. Then she had problems, and they had to take the babies early, and I was really worried. But I think the whole thing brought us closer together. When she was in the hospital, she nearly died. She showed me how strong she was. It was the scariest thing in my life, but it was a good experience for me, too. I would trade anything for her not to have had to go through with it.

I can honestly say that I never thought about abortion or adoption. I'm pro-choice—I think it's the woman's decision. It's her body and her life. But that wasn't for me. I'm the kind to tough it out. If we had decided on adoption, I'd always be wondering what does the kid look like. I wanted to love someone that's my own. I'm glad we made the choice we did.

I feel so much more grown up than I did this time last year. I look back at myself then and think, "I acted like such an idiot." I might have given up a little bit, but I gained more than I lost. I was planning on going to college, and I put that on hold. I want to be a respiratory therapist. In the fall I'll probably go to school part time instead of full time. I'll definitely do something. The babies were an inspiration for me to be better, to do something with my life. Now I put them first.

I've had to make some changes. I used to think nothing of spending a hundred dollars on a jacket or sneakers. Now I can't go out and spend a hundred dollars so easily, knowing that my kids need formula and diapers. And I can't go out with my friends, knowing that Janet's home with the babies.

When my parents found out, they were happy and scared, too, but they trusted me. They were upset, because they wanted me to go to college. But they've given me all the support I need.

I was afraid . . . you know, embarrassed to tell them at first. They always used to look at me, not like an angel, but I know they didn't think this would happen. I told my mom first. I listened to what she said, then I tried to do what was best. She knew that's what I'd do.

Around my neighborhood, I was always pretty popular. A lot of my friends felt sad for me when they found out, because they knew it meant that I wouldn't be able to do the things I normally do—you know, just hanging out. But I had people I didn't even know asking me about Janet and about the babies. It made me a little bit angry that they were talking about me. But really, I couldn't care less what people think.

I worried a little about getting Janet pregnant, but I guess I was always a little on the daring side. I thought, "That can't happen to me." That's where I didn't use my head.

If I was giving advice, I'd say, be sure you're prepared. It's your choice, but if you're gonna do it, be sure you're ready. For me, and for Janet, it was more right than wrong.

As far as having kids, I'd say wait until you're married, or at least more established. You should know your goals in life. At least wait until your early 20s.

It bothers me that we're not married, but we're too young. We didn't want to add any more pressure to the pressure we already have. I think if we got married now, it would make everything a lot more difficult. With the babies and all, it would be too much at once. I see marriage in our future when our lives get more established. We'll get to grow together. Right now, we have more to think about.

I had no fears that I wouldn't be a good parent. I have a younger brother and three younger sisters. But being a father is a lot more responsibility than being a big brother. My mom always made sure that my sisters were clothed and fed. I had the easy part—just playing with them.

The worst part of everything is the baby who's still in the hospital. She still might not have a chance. I can't get it off my mind. I'm so worried about it. It might be three years or it might be ten before we really know if she's going to be OK. She can take three steps forward today and ten back tomorrow. That adds so much pressure to the whole situation.

I'll be at work and the guys will say, "Why don't you call the hospital and see how the baby is doing?" I can call, but a phone call just isn't good enough.

I never thought that something like this would happen . . . you know, one of the babies being sick. It's like Janet being sick wasn't enough. But it's something you don't think about. My mother had five kids, and all of them were fine. My grandmother had six, and all of them were fine.

I guess it's a little bit easier having one of them home. I can look at her and know her sister's gonna get better. But she knows something's missing. They're close already. They spent all that time together. When Janet had ultrasound, we could see them touching each other. It was really neat.

The doctor saw that one of them had an umbilical hernia, but they said, "That's nothing. Don't worry about it." I guess I didn't think enough about what could happen. Even so, I wouldn't have done anything different.

Keeping the Baby

Q I just found out that I'm pregnant. I really want to keep the baby, but my parents don't think that I should. They say I'm too young. I'm 17. What do you think I should do?

A First of all, it's great that you could talk to your parents about your pregnancy. They might not agree with you, but they really will try to help you do what's best. As long as you all can keep talking—calmly and honestly—you can probably count on their support.

Second, have you told the baby's father? The decision is yours to make, but he should be involved, too. He was part of making that baby, and you need to know how ready he is to accept the responsibility for raising that child. His reaction might make a difference in helping you decide.

Whether or not you are too young to raise a baby really depends on you. Can you handle the demands that a baby places on you? Can you manage financially? Are you ready for the hard work and the changes to your life?

• • • • • • • • • • • •

Having a baby involves a lot more than what that simple phrase implies. It sounds so easy—like "having a party" or "getting a pet." But having a baby isn't simple. Think of it as being a parent—as taking on a 20-year job. A parent needs to meet all of a child's needs:

■ Providing food, clothing, and shelter

■ Teaching right and wrong, how to cooperate with others, and how to treat other people

■ Providing nursing care in times of illness

■ Being there at all times to listen, offer suggestions, and provide help

Parenting is hard work. But, of course, it isn't all hard work. Ask your parents. They'll probably tell you that parenthood is one of the most rewarding experiences of their lives. There are lots of happy times and fun. But entering this new stage means making major adjustments. A teen's entire life changes once a child is born. Let's look at what being a parent is like.

Reality Check: Life with a Baby

The idea of having a cuddly, cooing baby to love you and depend on you can be very appealing. But the key word here is *depend*. An infant is totally dependent on adults for *everything*. Babies need to be fed, burped, changed, bathed, or held almost around the clock. They can make these needs known in only one way: crying. When a parent hears a baby's cry, no matter what time it is, he or she needs to respond with help. Sometimes settling a baby back down at night can take a long time.

The first few months—when the new parent first faces all these demands—can be overwhelming. That's what Angela thought. "I'd never been so tired in my whole life. Keith didn't sleep through the night until he was six months old! Every night it was the same thing. He'd wake up sometime between 12:00 and 1:00 for a feeding. He'd be real upset, crying real loud, and it would take him almost an hour to settle down. Then I could finally feed him. Then when he was done, he wanted to play! I tried putting him back in his crib, but he'd scream. He usually wouldn't go back to sleep until 3:30 or 4:00. By then, I was so wound up, it took me a while to sleep again. And by 7:00, he was up all over again to start the day."

Life settles down a bit when middle-of-the-night feedings stop, but it is never the same as before the baby. When a teen mother has to take full responsibility, it can seem unbearable.

The new mother's days change as well. No plans can be made without providing for the baby. A shopping trip can become a major expedition—with diaper bag, stroller, toys, a bottle, and a change of clothes. Many teen mothers miss being able to drop everything to go out with friends. Some can get a parent or grandparent to watch the baby while they go out, and sometimes friends can come over to visit. But there are days when a teen mother's life is a lonely one.

Children are expensive, too. Babies need new clothes as they grow—and they grow rapidly in the first year. They need clean diapers many times a day, and those cost money, too. Teen parents often need help managing the financial burdens of raising a child. Sometimes their parents can provide that help. If the baby's father helps, the situation is a little easier.

Health Issues

A pregnant teen who wants to keep her baby has to act carefully during the pregnancy so that the baby is healthy when it is born. Good prenatal care is the key.

Pregnancy puts heavy physical demands on a woman's body. It is especially demanding on a teenager, whose own body is still growing and developing. For this reason, teens run a higher-than-average risk of having serious complications with pregnancy and childbirth. These potential problems can threaten their lives or the baby's. Fortunately, pregnant teens can take steps to ensure that they behave in healthful ways. Getting enough rest and having some exercise are two of those steps. But the three that follow are the most important:

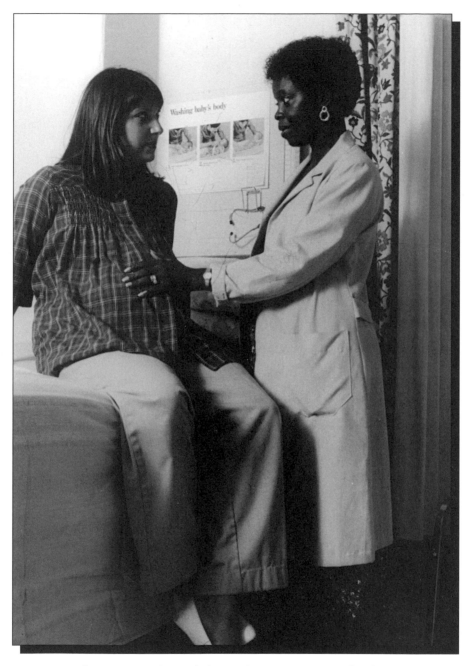

Pregnancy places many physical demands on a teenage girl, whose body is still growing. It is extremely important that she see her doctor regularly.

- Getting regular checkups by a doctor

- Eating a balanced diet

- Avoiding drugs

Regular Checkups

Seeing a doctor regularly is the first step toward a healthy pregnancy. Visits usually take place once a month for the first few months, then become more frequent as the due date nears. The doctor examines the mother-to-be and determines the baby's growth since the last visit. In later stages of the pregnancy, he or she will listen to the baby's heartbeat for signs of possible problems. Doctors give advice and suggestions at these visits. Checkups also provide the mother with an opportunity to ask about anything that's bothering her physically or emotionally about the pregnancy.

Healthy Diet

Good nutrition is crucial to the health of both mother and baby. It includes two important parts: eating enough calories and eating a well-balanced diet.

A teen who is pregnant must eat more than a teen who isn't pregnant. That can be a real problem for some girls. Our society prizes slimness, and teen girls are often weight conscious. When they are pregnant, though, teens cannot skimp on their eating just to avoid gaining weight. Doing so can endanger their health and the baby's.

The second part of good nutrition is eating a balanced diet that will provide all the vitamins and minerals that both mother and baby need. Feasting on fries and ice cream adds calories, but not nutrients. The doctor will probably make some recommendations for a healthful diet.

Avoiding Drugs

Anything that a pregnant teen swallows, smokes, snorts, or

injects enters the baby's body. The baby can be seriously harmed when the mother:

■ Drinks alcohol

■ Smokes cigarettes

■ Smokes, swallows, snorts, or shoots illegal drugs

■ Takes caffeine (found in coffee, tea, cola, and many diet pills)

■ Uses any medicines, including aspirin

Doctors recommend against taking any of these substances in any amount while pregnant. Even common over-the-counter drugs, such as aspirin, are advised against without a specific OK from the doctor.

The more powerful substances—alcohol, tobacco, and illegal drugs—are especially damaging to the baby. They can cause a wide range of problems, including low birth weight, miscarriage, deformities, and mental retardation. Some babies are born addicted to these substances, starting their lives off tragically. *Drugs and pregnancy do not mix.*

The Role of the Father

The baby's father can participate in raising the child from the beginning. Some fathers take an active role during the pregnancy. They visit the doctor along with the mother, learning about how the baby develops and grows during pregnancy.

Fathers can join the mother in prepared childbirth classes, too. These classes, conducted by public health nurses, provide important information about labor and delivery. In them, expectant mothers learn what will happen when labor begins and the actual birth occurs. The classes include practice in breathing and relaxation techniques that can help the mother handle the pain of labor. Fathers learn to coach the mother

Many teenage fathers take an active role in the pregnancy. Having two parents to care for the child makes the job easier.

through the process. In most cases, they can even be present in the delivery room at birth. Many fathers feel that watching their child being born is a high point in their lives.

Having two parents to care for the child makes the job easier. If the baby is fed formula, both mother and father can take turns giving nighttime feedings. That cuts down on the sleepless nights for either parent. Many fathers feel closer to their children when they take part in caring for them.

Some fathers choose not to get involved. That decision means that they miss out on the joy of raising a child and watching him or her grow and learn. This choice also puts an added burden on the teen mother. She can try to get the father to accept financial responsibility for the child by taking him to court. She can also turn to parents or social agencies for help.

Teen Parents and Schooling

Choosing to become a teen parent affects the rest of a teen's life, but it doesn't necessarily end all hopes and dreams. A teen mother may have to give up—or postpone—some of her goals. She may have to achieve some in different ways than originally planned.

The same is true of a teen father. A father at 19, Frank realized that he didn't have the time or money to afford medical school, as he'd planned. Instead he entered an allied health program. There he learned to be a physical therapist while working part time in a local hospital. With this training, he was still able to work in health care, the field he wanted. Although he is earning much less than he would have earned as a physician, he was able to get a full-time job sooner and with less expensive training.

The father can usually finish high school without interruption, unless he needs to take a full-time job to help meet expenses. It's a good idea to stay in school. He'll have more job options in the future if he graduates.

The teen mother will probably have to take a break in schooling at some point in her pregnancy. She may feel too nauseated or tired to stay in school all day. She may be able to

A pregnant teen can usually remain in school as long as she is able. Many high schools offer classes in childbirth and parenting.

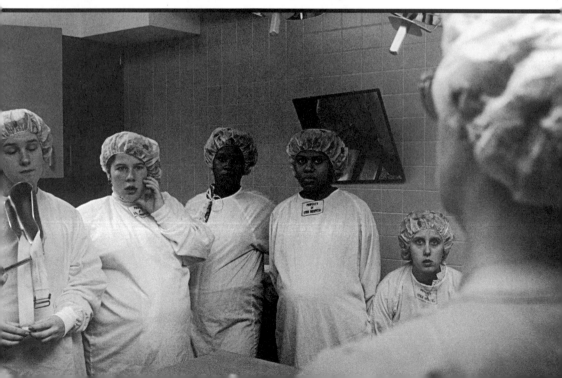

Many teen couples marry because the girl is pregnant. As with most marriages, it takes commitment, caring, and communication to make them last.

attend until late in the pregnancy, when the due date is near. Even if she has to stop school for a while, tutoring and studying at home may be available. The school guidance counselor will have information about those possibilities.

How quickly the mother can get back to school to get her diploma depends on how well she feels after the baby is born and how much support she gets. If someone is available to provide full-time child care, she can probably return as early as six weeks after delivery. Most teen mothers, though, must juggle full-time motherhood with part-time schooling. It's still possible to graduate—it just might take a while.

Both mother and father can go on to college, too, though that's largely a question of time and finances. Sometimes the father works during the day and takes classes at night. Once he's earned his degree, the mother might go on to college.

Marriage or Not

Whether to marry or not is a question that many teens face. Both options are difficult. It's hard for a teen mother to live alone. But marriage isn't always easy, and teen parents have many hurdles to overcome. The average teenager's financial situation is usually unstable, and the couple may live with one partner's parents until they can get on their feet.

Each year, about 100,000 teenage couples get married when

the girl is pregnant. Some of these marriages last. But it takes commitment, caring, and communication to make them work.

Many teens who marry don't really know each other well. And teens go through so many changes in their lives that the views and needs of either partner may change over time. In the everyday stresses of marriage, they may find that they don't love each other. They may feel trapped and resentful. That's a painful situation for both of them—and for the child, too.

Emilie went through a bad marriage. She really loved Jordan when they were going together. He was older, he had already graduated from high school, and he had a job. When she became pregnant and they agreed to marry, she was happier than she could imagine. But things didn't work out. "Jordan never stayed at home. He'd go out with his friends right after work. He'd come back late, and a lot of times he was drunk. When the baby cried, he'd yell at me, 'Shut the kid up.'"

Emilie tried to make the marriage work. "But it seemed that I couldn't do anything right. Jordan was always angry when he was around, but most of the time he wasn't there. He started hitting me. I was scared what he'd do to me—and to the baby." After two years, Emilie couldn't take it anymore. She received help at a shelter for battered women and eventually moved there with her baby.

Single parents are much more common today than ever before. Many communities have support groups that can help teen mothers adjust to their new lives. These groups offer the mothers a chance to share feelings with others in the same situation. These groups can be found in the local phone book or through the library.

A pregnant teen who decides to keep her baby faces a hard road. Raising a child offers many wonderful experiences—the baby's first smile, the first time he or she says "mama," and those first halting steps. But it also means a lot of hard work. The decision to keep a child should not be made without recognizing the difficulties as well as the joys of parenthood.

Adoption

Q I can't imagine being pregnant for nine months, going through labor and everything, then never seeing my baby or knowing what happened to it. If I go through with the adoption, will I ever be able to forget my baby?

A No one ever forgets. But most people feel positive about their choice in the long run, even though they may feel sad at first. It takes a mature and unselfish person to let someone else raise her child. Not everyone can do it. The counselors and case workers at adoption centers are trained to help you decide if adoption is right for you.

There are a few adoption and child-care situations that will let you maintain contact with your child as he or she grows up. Even so, you will not have any legal rights to that child if you go through with the adoption. Once the adoption is final, you can't change your mind. That's why it is so important to get as much information as you can before you make your choice.

• • • • • • • • • • •

Adoption is a legal process that gives a child new parents. The adoptive parents become the child's legal parents, and the child gets a new birth certificate. The birth parents, or biological parents, give up all parental rights to the child permanently.

Through adoption, couples who are unable to raise their child are matched with couples who can. Very often couples seek to adopt a child because they cannot have one of their own, but this isn't always the case. Some may already have other biological or adopted children. People have many different reasons for wanting to adopt—just as people have many reasons for wanting to find an adoptive home for their child.

Choosing Adoption

Many teens decide to keep their babies. Still each year, about 20,000 teens in the United States place their babies in adoptive homes. They feel that adoption is the best choice for them and for their baby.

"I just couldn't have an abortion. I think it's wrong," said Julia, who was 15 when she became pregnant. "And my boyfriend Tim only offered to marry me because he thought it was the right thing to do. I think he was relieved when I said I wanted to give the baby up for adoption. So were our parents. I couldn't see putting my mom through raising another child, and I knew I couldn't do it on my own."

Like many teens, Julia didn't feel that she was ready for marriage and parenthood, and she didn't want to burden her parents with a baby. Most teens can't handle the financial responsibilities of a baby, and their families won't or can't afford to help. Some teens decide that early parenthood will make it difficult or impossible to reach their life goals. Some teens would have preferred to end the pregnancy, but waited too long to make that decision and then found that it was too late for a safe, legal abortion.

Counseling is important for a couple considering placing their child in an adoptive home. Social workers and adoption counselors can explain the couple's options. They want to make sure that the birth parents understand that adoption is permanent and that they can't change their minds once the adoption is final. They can also help the birth parents handle the feelings of loss and sadness that may follow the adoption.

Some states allow a grace period between signing the consent forms and finalizing the adoption. This period may last from ten days to a few months. During this time, the birth parents may be able to take the baby back from the adoptive parents. If the adoptive parents challenge the request, the issue goes before a judge. Judges frequently decide that the baby should live with its birth parent or parents. After the grace period is over, however, the court usually won't take the baby away from adoptive parents. Even very young infants become emotionally attached to their caregivers. And it is upsetting to them to be moved back and forth between different sets of parents. The court will rule on what is best for the child.

Adoption laws vary from state to state. Most states require both birth parents to sign the adoption papers. Therefore, the couple should discuss adoption as soon as possible to prevent problems later.

Kinds of Adoptions

Adoptions are arranged in several different ways. Usually they are made through a state-licensed adoption agency or privately, through an attorney. Parents can arrange adoptions at any time, but most often they are done before the baby is born for several reasons. First, it is easier to find adoptive parents for a newborn than for an older child. Second, it is upsetting for the child to be taken from the parents he or she has come to depend on. Third, it's much harder for the birth parents if the separation comes after they've come to know their baby for a while.

Traditional Adoption
In a traditional adoption, the adoption agency finds, screens, and selects the adoptive parents, and makes all the arrangements. Social workers interview potential adoptive couples and check their background. They may talk with people who

know the couple, such as coworkers or members of their religious organization. They will visit the couple's home to evaluate the environment. The agency wants to know that the couple is emotionally and financially stable.

The agency can provide counseling and support groups for the birth parents and their families, and prenatal education for the birth mother. The agency can sometimes arrange for financial help for the birth mother's medical expenses, if necessary. It can sometimes arrange for foster care if the birth mother needs a place to stay during her pregnancy.

After a traditional adoption is finalized, the baby is issued a new birth certificate, and all other records are sealed. The birth parents have no further contact with the baby, and they do not know the identity of the adoptive parents. This process may raise some questions for an adopted child later in life—questions about why their birth parents chose adoption or about their family's medical history.

The total separation of a traditional adoption may be difficult for the birth parents as well. "My old girlfriend gave our baby up for adoption nine years ago," said Mark, who became a father for the first time at age 17. Now he's married to someone else, and they have a 3-year-old son. "It hurts a little every time I look at Josh, because I think of my first son. I never even saw him. I wonder if he has my eyes, too, like Josh does. I hope

If keeping the baby is not an option for a pregnant teen, adoption may be a suitable alternative. Approximately 500,000 children were adopted in the United States in 1991.

he's having a happy life. If I knew that, it would be worth it."

Some states allow adoption records to be unsealed at the child's request after he or she has turned 18. Some adopted children seek out their biological parents. Sometimes these reunions are joyful. Other such meetings are awkward and painful, because the parent and child are strangers.

Open Adoption

Today many birth parents help to choose the adoptive parents. Agencies that arrange open adoptions keep files of letters, applications, and videotapes of couples seeking adoption. Birth parents can review these materials and meet with potential adoptive parents before the baby is born. Sometimes the adoptive parents come to the hospital at the time of the baby's birth.

Afterward the adoptive parents send the birth parents regular reports on the child's progress as he or she grows up. Many birth parents say that they felt reassured by meeting the adoptive parents. Sometimes the birth parents and the adoptive parents maintain a close relationship because of their mutual concern for the child. The success of an open adoption depends on the people involved and their understanding of the role they have in the child's life. Open adoptions also enable the adoptive family to learn more about the birth family.

Charlene, age 20, chose to stay in touch with the couple who adopted her daughter four years ago. "Emma lives with her adoptive parents a few hours away, on the other side of the state. They're really great people," said Charlene. "I visited them a few times when I had the money for the bus fare. It's hard not to think of Emma as my daughter, but she only knows me as a friend of the family. When I see how happy she is, though, I know I did the right thing. She has a room of her own and a big yard to play in. The house is in a really nice neighborhood. I could never have given her all that." Charlene is happy with her decision, and understands she can't take an active role in Emma's life at this time.

Private Adoption

It's not necessary to go through an agency to arrange an adoption. Sometimes the adoption is arranged through the birth mother's doctor and an attorney who specializes in adoption or family law. A private adoption is usually quicker and easier than an agency adoption. However, potential adoptive parents may not be screened as carefully as they are for an agency adoption. If a private adoption is being considered, the parties involved should make certain that the procedure is legally recorded and that the adoption papers are filed at the appropriate county office.

Illegal Adoption

There's a big demand for healthy babies to adopt. Many couples wait for years before a baby becomes available for them to adopt. Some grow so desperate that they are willing to pay any price to adopt a child. Through a doctor, lawyer, or other go-between, they offer the pregnant teen a lot of money for the baby. This is buying and selling a baby, and it is *illegal!* No papers are kept, and the adoptive parents aren't screened. Although the money may be attractive, these "underground" adoptions don't protect the birth parents' legal rights, and they may place the child at risk.

Foster Care

Although foster care isn't a permanent solution, it does provide teen parents with another option. With foster care, the parents agree to let someone else care for their child until they can do it themselves. Foster care is temporary. It gives the teen parent time to finish school, get a job, find a place to live, or whatever it takes to be able to care for the baby. Then the baby goes to live with its birth parent or parents.

Both parents must agree to a foster care arrangement. Sometimes the foster parent is a relative or a friend of the family, and the agreement is informal. In these cases, the birth parents still have a legal right to the child. In other cases, a social service agency finds the foster home, and a formal agreement is signed. This makes the agency legally responsible for the child's care. The agency doesn't need the parents' permission to place the baby in a different home or make other decisions about the baby's care. The child might be placed in a private home or a group facility.

Foster care is a voluntary agreement. The only exception occurs when the birth parent acts irresponsibly while the baby is in foster care. Getting involved with drugs or alcohol, getting into trouble with the law, or not maintaining contact with the baby are some of the reasons that might prevent birth parents from regaining custody of their child. As in adoption, if the issue goes to court, the judge will determine what is in the child's best interest.

Sometimes mother and baby go into a foster home together. The foster family helps the teen mother with her baby until she can manage by herself.

Social service agencies have information about the different types of adoptions and foster care available to teen parents. It's important to understand what the options are before making this serious life decision. Seeking information and counseling from an adoption agency does not commit the birth parents to arranging an adoption. However, such counseling will help them decide whether adoption is the best choice for them and for the child.

Abortion

Q My girlfriend is pregnant. She wants an abortion, but I think she should keep the baby. Don't I get a say in what happens to my kid?

A It's really good that you aren't walking away from this pregnancy that you helped to create. The fact that you want to be involved in the decision shows a great deal of maturity. But are you ready for the physical, emotional, and financial demands of parenting? It sounds like your girlfriend isn't ready to take on that full-time responsibility of raising this child. Tell her how you feel and listen carefully to what she says. Let her make the decision. She's the one who will carry the baby for nine months and face the risks of childbirth. If she decides to have an abortion, she will need as much support as you can give her for the next few weeks, even if you don't agree with her decision.

You're probably having a tough time dealing with your feelings right now—and your girlfriend may be too involved in her own problems to help. Try talking to someone you trust—a parent, a teacher, your family doctor, or an abortion counselor.

• • • • • • • • • • •

Abortion is a very controversial topic; people have strong opinions on the issue—for or against. But for the couple deal-

Although women in the United States currently have the right to choose to end a pregnancy, there may be obstacles to overcome in order to have an abortion. In this photo, supporters on both sides of the abortion issue demonstrate in front of a Massachusetts clinic.

ing with an unplanned pregnancy, the issue may not be so black and white. Making the decision is difficult when it becomes personal. No one really wants to make the decision to end a pregnancy, even if they want the right to make that choice.

Making the Decision

People usually don't think about how they would handle a pregnancy—until they are actually faced with one. Even if they have given it some thought beforehand, their feelings can change when the pregnancy becomes a reality. Now they have to make a serious decision when they may be feeling angry, scared, proud, and excited all at once. It helps to talk about these conflicting emotions with someone who understands.

For her own sake, a pregnant woman who chooses an abortion must know that she is the one making the decision. She has to feel comfortable with her decision. Physicians do not want to perform abortions on women who will have regrets about ending the pregnancy.

Tracy was 15 when she became pregnant. Both she and her boyfriend agreed that they were too young to get married. Besides, Tracy was raised in a strictly religious family. She was afraid of what her parents would do when they found out that she was having sex with her boyfriend. Even though she was raised to believe that abortion is wrong, she thought that having an abortion would be easier than telling her parents she was pregnant.

"I was so confused," Tracy said. "The more I talked with the counselor at the abortion clinic, the more I realized I couldn't go through with it. I just couldn't live with myself if I had the abortion."

The counselor coached Tracy through breaking the news to her parents. As Tracy expected, they were shocked and upset at first. But she was surprised at how supportive they became.

"They went with me to different adoption agencies. I think we were all relieved that abortion wasn't the only option," she recalled.

Not all young women are like Tracy. Many do not believe that abortion is wrong. For them, abortion may be a positive choice and far less traumatic than giving birth to an unwanted child. Some people who oppose abortion say that women who have abortions suffer from emotional problems afterward, but this is generally not true. It's natural to feel some sadness after ending a pregnancy, and each person handles it differently. According to researchers at The Alan Guttmacher Institute, women who have abortions usually feel relieved.

A teenager who is considering abortion should make her decision as early as possible. The earlier an abortion is done, the safer it is. Abortions done in the first trimester, the first 12 weeks after the woman's last menstrual period, are the safest. Abortions later in a pregnancy are more complicated and sometimes more difficult to obtain.

Legal Issues

In 1973, the United States Supreme Court legalized abortion with a decision in the case of *Roe* v. *Wade*. Some people would like to see that decision reversed. But for now, women have the right to choose to end a pregnancy. However, the laws vary from state to state. Almost all states require that a licensed physician perform the abortion, although Vermont allows other licensed health-care providers to perform the procedure. Most states do not allow abortions in the third trimester unless the mother's life is in danger. Some states, such as Pennsylvania, North Dakota, Kansas, and Arkansas, require that girls under 18 get permission for an abortion from one or both of their parents. Generally, those states will allow the pregnant teen to get court approval in place of parental permission.

Caroline and Chris always used foam, but no other contraceptive. This time it wasn't enough. "When I got pregnant, Chris and I had a long talk about our futures. We decided that I'd get an abortion," Caroline said.

But it wasn't that easy. Their state law required permission from both of Caroline's parents. Chris recalled, "Caroline didn't know what to do. A few months earlier, her mother caught us kissing. She really lost it. She called Caroline a slut and threw a shoe at her."

"My father has an even worse temper," Caroline added. Caroline was scared and upset when she discovered that she was pregnant. She called an abortion clinic, explained her problem, and made an appointment to talk with a counselor. They discussed Caroline's home situation, her goals for the future, and her options for dealing with the pregnancy. The counselor told Caroline that a judge could give her permission for the abortion. Caroline thought about it for several days and decided she wanted an abortion. The counselor then helped her set up the appointment with a judge. The judge asked Caroline some questions about her family life and her decision to have an abortion. The judge, convinced that Caroline had given the matter serious thought, gave her the forms that she needed.

Choosing a Clinic

As with any medical procedure, choosing the right health-care provider is important. If a woman feels comfortable with the clinic or hospital, and the people who work there, she'll be a lot more relaxed about the procedure. In choosing a doctor or facility, she should not be reluctant to call several places and to ask a lot of questions. Here are some sample questions:

■ Is counseling available before and after the abortion? Is it private counseling or group counseling?

■ Can a friend come along for support? Can he or she witness the procedure?

■ Will an anesthetic be used? What kind? Will there be any aftereffects from the anesthesia?

■ Would you describe the procedure for me? Will it be painful?

■ Will I be required to stay overnight?

■ How much will the abortion cost? Will my medical insurance cover it? If so, can you help me with the paperwork? Will I need money up front or can I arrange a payment plan?

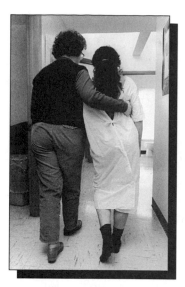

Frequently counselors will accompany and support a teenager about to have an abortion.

The appointment should be made with the doctor or facility that best meets the teen's needs and means.

Once that appointment has been made, the doctor will give instructions about preparing for the abortion, for example, not eating anything after midnight. They should be followed exactly. Before the operation, the doctor will usually do a pelvic examination to confirm that the woman is still pregnant. As with any medical procedure, she will also be given a consent form to sign.

Types of Abortions

There are several different ways to end a pregnancy. The type of abortion that is recommended depends on how long the woman has been pregnant, or how long since her last menstrual period.

Vacuum Suction

The most common type is vacuum suction. This kind of abortion is done only when the woman is less than 12 weeks pregnant. The entire procedure generally takes about 10 minutes and can be done in a clinic or hospital. The patient is awake during the procedure. Some patients are given a tranquilizer to help ease any discomfort.

During the vacuum suction procedure, the physician opens the woman's vagina with a speculum, the same instrument that is used for the pelvic exam. He or she will inject a local anesthetic to numb the cervix. The doctor then uses a dilator to open the cervix. This may cause some cramping. After the cervix is dilated, the doctor inserts a narrow, flexible tube into the uterus and carefully suctions out the embryo or fetus and the uterine lining.

Aimee was relieved because she wasn't pregnant anymore. She had been terrified about the pregnancy, about the abortion, and about how she was going to feel afterward. Aimee talked with a counselor about birth control before she went home.

"Even though the actual abortion was much easier than I expected, I never want to go through all that again," Aimee said—and she meant it.

A girl who has an abortion can become pregnant again. However, girls who have repeated abortions run the risk of having problems later on when they decide they are ready to have a child.

Dilation and Curettage

Because the fetus is larger and more developed, abortions after the first trimester are more complicated. From 12 to 16 weeks, doctors will use dilation and curettage, sometimes called a D and C, to terminate a pregnancy.

To perform dilation and curettage, the doctor will use a series of dilators to open the cervix. Then he or she will insert a thin spoon-shaped instrument, called a curette, to loosen and to scrape tissue from the wall of the uterus.

Dilation and curettage can be done in a doctor's office with local anesthetic, but more often it is done in a hospital while the patient is under general anesthetic. The procedure takes about 30 minutes. Recently, doctors have been using a procedure called dilation and evacuation, which combines vacuum suction with dilation and curettage.

Induced Abortion

By the end of the second trimester, abortions can be especially risky and difficult. They also require a 24- to 48-hour hospital stay. It is rare that an abortion is performed at this stage in a pregnancy. Many physicians will not perform them unless the pregnancy puts the mother's life in danger.

By this stage in the pregnancy, the fetus is well-developed. To end the pregnancy, the doctor injects a saline solution or a hormone called prostaglandin into the amniotic fluid, which surrounds the fetus. After a few hours, the uterus begins to contract. The contractions cause the cervix to dilate and the fetus and placenta to be expelled. This process can be very painful and can take several hours. It is similar to labor and childbirth.

Aftercare

Sometimes after an abortion, a woman may be depressed—especially in the first 72 hours. There will be some bleeding, discomfort (similar to menstrual cramps), and general weakness. The doctor or a nurse will give the patient important instructions to prevent infection or other complications. Some of the danger signs to watch for are the following:

■ Fever or chills

■ Severe abdominal pain

- Excessive bleeding (heavier than a normal period)

- Foul-smelling vaginal discharge

- Continuing symptoms of pregnancy

A women who experiences any of these symptoms should notify her doctor immediately. Even if there are no problems, a woman who has had an abortion should have a further followup examination by her doctor about two weeks after the procedure.

Medical experts agree that abortions performed by properly trained and licensed professionals are usually very safe, particularly if they're done very early in the pregnancy. "Back alley" abortions, done by untrained and/or unlicensed people, are *dangerous* and *illegal*. Don't even think about it! They can lead to sterility or even death. The same is true for self-induced abortions. What's more, they usually don't work, and they could do irreparable harm to the fetus.

Some Last Words

It is normal for one or both partners to feel some sadness or a sense of loss after an abortion. For the girl, this may be the result of hormonal changes as her body adjusts to not being pregnant anymore. But both teens have been through a major emotional event, and they are bound to experience a lot of different emotions. Professional counseling can help both partners to deal with their problems and concerns and help them move on with their lives.

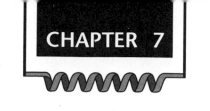

Special Issues

Q After we went to the movies one night, my friend and I went back to his house. His parents weren't home. Before I had time to think about it, we were having sex. I didn't really want to, but I went along with it. Now, I'm sorry I did. What went wrong?

A Maybe a better question to ask yourself would be, "Why do I feel this way and what would make me feel better about myself?"

Having sex almost always stirs up a lot of complicated emotions. You may feel ashamed or angry with yourself or your friend. You need to stop feeling bad about yourself, or you may find yourself in a situation like this again.

If you haven't already, now is a good time to take a close look at your feelings about sex. When do you feel it's right? What does it mean to you? When you're sure about your own feelings, it's easier to communicate those feelings to others. In the long run, you'll feel more positive about yourself and people will respect you.

• • • • • • • • • • • •

So far, we've talked about situations in which two people agreed to have sex. Unfortunately, that's not always how it happens. Young people often have mixed feelings about having sex. Sometimes one person may try to coerce—by verbal argument or physical force—the other person to have sex when he or she doesn't want to. If the sex act takes place when only one participant wants it, the result can be emotional or physical wounds that may take a long time to heal.

Reasons to Say "No"

Any person can say "no" to sex at any time. Some of the reasons a person might choose to abstain from having sex include:

- moral or religious beliefs
- lack of birth control
- lack of a condom for disease control
- fatigue
- worry about privacy
- lack of romantic feeling for the other person
- headache
- worry about the consequences

Feeling uneasy about the situation, the setting, the timing, or the other person is enough reason not to have sex at that particular moment. People who care about each other will respect each other's decisions.

Rape

Unfortunately, sometimes sex has nothing to do with love. It doesn't even have anything to do with being attracted to someone. For some people, sex is a way of expressing anger and hatred and of wielding power over someone. Forcing someone to have sex is called rape.

Most people think of a rapist as a stranger lurking in a dark alley, jumping out and sexually attacking a woman. This does happen, and the experience can be both frightening and humiliating.

A woman who is raped should seek medical help immediately. She may have injuries, such as cuts or broken bones, that need attention. A hospital emergency-room physician will also check for internal injuries that might not be obvious. The victim should also be tested for pregnancy as well as sexually transmitted diseases immediately after the rape and at a follow-up visit a few weeks later. If the woman decides to take legal action later, the hospital will have the medical records.

A rape should be reported to the police immediately—whether or not the victim is going to pursue the case. By reporting the rape right away, a record of the incident is established. If there is no record, the rape victim will have difficulty pressing charges later.

Acquaintance Rape

Few rapes involve strangers and deserted alleys. More than half of reported rapes are committed by someone the woman knows. This is called "acquaintance rape" or "date rape." Any time a man uses physical force or another kind of pressure to have sex with a woman, it is rape.

One reason for the occurrence of date rape is that people have certain expectations about male and female roles in society. For instance, many people think that men are supposed to be macho and aggressive and that women are supposed to be passive. Some also think that women often say "no" when they really mean "yes." This kind of thinking leads to serious misunderstandings. The truth is, it won't hurt a man's masculinity if he doesn't have sex. And when most women say "no" or "stop," that's exactly what they mean.

The responsibility for avoiding date rape belongs to both

Avoiding Date Rape

To Minimize Chances of Becoming a Date Rape Victim:

❑ Find out about a person before being alone with him.

❑ Socialize with people who share your values.

❑ Learn to take care of yourself. Don't assume that there will be someone around to come to your rescue.

❑ Stay away from boys (people) who seem insensitive, bossy, jealous, competitive, or short-tempered.

❑ Be careful about being alone with a date in your room or home or his. A date rape is most likely to occur in a victim's or assailant's home.

❑ Be assertive. Set limits at the beginning of a date.

❑ Avoid secluded places, especially at the beginning of a relationship.

❑ Be aware that the use of alcohol or drugs is often associated with date rape.

Sources: *Wide Awake: A Guide to Safe Campus Living in the 90's*, M.C. and M.D. Smith, Peterson's Guides, 1990; *Coping with Date Rape and Acquaintance Rape*, Andrea Parrot, Rosen, 1988; *The Facts About Rape*, J.B. Guernsey, Crestwood House, 1990.

Date rape leaves people feeling angry and ashamed. By clearly communicating your limits and avoiding secluded places, you can avoid becoming a victim.

people. Teenagers need to examine their feelings about sex carefully and set their own limits. They're allowed to change those limits as relationships change. What may seem inappropriate at the beginning of a relationship can become less so as the relationship strengthens and matures. Each situation is different, even if the same two people are involved.

Communication about sex is extremely important—and often difficult. Couples should not assume that they know what their date's intentions are—or that their own wishes are obvious. It may be embarrassing to talk about sex at first. But in the long run, it is better than allowing something that you didn't want to happen.

Listening is as important as talking for both of the teens involved. Sometimes the other person is very clear about what he or she wants, as Diane found out on a date with Dale.

"All through dinner, Dale kept telling me how beautiful I was, how sexy I looked. At first I was very flattered, so I didn't think about what he was really saying," Diane recalled.

"We were alone back at his parents' house and started kissing. He told me how much he wanted to make love to me," she continued. "Looking back, I don't know why I didn't realize he meant that night. Well, the situation got out of hand. He got what he wanted, but I wouldn't call it making love."

Body language is also important. The signals you send with your actions can be a source of confusion if they don't reflect how you really feel. If a boy sees a girl in sexy clothes, he may think that means she wants to have sex, no matter what she says. Being flirtatious or even kissing may seem like a signal that the person wants to have intercourse. Maybe the person only wants to be friendly or get some attention. No one deserves to be forced into sex for that.

Two Sides

Girls have a responsibility, too. They need to understand how boys might misunderstand their actions.

"I don't understand what Diane got so mad about," said Dale. "I mean, she was wearing a low-cut sweater and tight jeans, and she looked hot. She seemed pretty pleased when I told her that, too. All during dinner she kept leaning over toward me and touching my arm. Back at my parents' house, she really got into it. All of a sudden, she starts saying `no,' but she didn't move away or anything, so I thought she wanted me to try harder. That's what I did. How was I supposed to know she didn't want to go all the way?"

Staying in public places is a good way to avoid ugly situations.

Dale and Diane got into an ugly situation for two reasons. First, Diane's body language was telling Dale to go ahead, even though she wasn't ready to have intercourse with him. Second, when Diane did speak up and say "stop," Dale didn't listen.

One major way people can prevent date rape is to avoid excessive drinking or drugs. Alcohol and drugs can interfere with clear thinking and communication. Those same few drinks that can coax a shy teenager onto the dance floor can loosen his or her inhibitions about other things, too. They can temporarily stop teens from thinking about the consequences of their actions. A lot of people regret many things that happen when they're drunk or high, as Kristin learned the hard way.

"I was at a big party at the shore over spring break. There was so much beer! There was this guy there from the football team that I had a crush on. After a couple of beers, I finally got up the nerve to talk to him," said Kristin, a senior-year honor student.

"He said he was glad I talked to him, 'cause he always wanted to meet me. He told me that he could tell I wasn't like a lot of other girls. I guess that's what I wanted to hear that night, because when it was over, I wasn't a virgin anymore," she said.

"The really rotten thing is, he never called me after that. I feel so cheap. And I know if I hadn't been drunk, I wouldn't have had sex with him," Kristin added.

Sexual Abuse

The boy at the party took advantage of the fact that Kristin was drunk. Even though she never said "no" to sex, she wouldn't have had sex with him if she hadn't been drinking. There are other situations in which a person has sex with someone who isn't able to say "no." Taking advantage of someone like this is called sexual abuse.

Like date rape, sexual abuse isn't necessarily violent, but it is very upsetting. The victim usually knows and trusts the abuser. Sex abusers take advantage of people who are much younger or weaker than they are. Their actions may range from taking the victim's clothes off, to fondling or oral sex, to vaginal or anal penetration. When this happens between two members of the same family who aren't married, it is called incest. Like other types of rape, incest is a crime.

When they're very young, sisters and brothers often explore each other's bodies. This natural curiosity usually is harmless. But sometimes teens may sexually abuse younger children— either siblings or family friends. The most commonly reported type of incest involves a father, stepfather, uncles, or mother's boyfriend and daughter.

Regardless of age or relationship to the abuser, the victim usually feels powerless. The victim may feel that he or she wouldn't be believed, or that somehow he or she deserves what is happening. In many cases, the victim both loves and fears the abuser.

If the abuse goes on for a long time, it can hurt the victim's ability to trust people or to develop healthy sexual relationships. Very often, the victim of incest or other sexual abuse abuses others physically, sexually, or emotionally later in life.

What to Do

A victim of rape, incest, or other sexual abuse needs help. Confiding in a family member is a good start. A rape crisis center, a hot line, or community mental health center can provide support for those who are afraid to turn to family members. These are listed in the phone book.

The victim may be very angry. She may be scared. She may feel dirty and disgusting, or she may feel guilty and ashamed. It's important for the victim and those around her to remember that the rape or abuse was not her fault. A trained counselor can help a victim overcome the painful feelings that follow a rape or sexual abuse.

Remember that any unprotected sexual acts can lead to pregnancy or transmission of disease. And, as mentioned earlier, a medical exam could provide important documentation in case the victim decides to press charges later.

Some women don't press charges because they are afraid of their attacker or they want to keep the rape a secret. Some are afraid that they will be the ones on trial—and often that's what it feels like. On the other hand, some women feel that pressing charges helps them deal with their anger. It may also keep a rapist from raping again.

The decision to become sexually active is a serious one, and one that creates certain responsibilities. Facing an unplanned pregnancy requires other serious decisions. This book does not make those decisions for you. Instead, we have tried to provide vital information to help you make that decision in a mature and informed way. Read this book, ask for advice from people you respect, assess your options, and then make your decision based on what is best for you at this time in your life.

Several people can provide you with more information about sexuality, pregnancy, and sexually transmitted diseases. Your family doctor or school nurse would be glad to help you. Another good resource is a family planning clinic, such as Planned Parenthood. You can find family planning clinics in the phone book under "family services," "pregnancy counseling," or "sex-related concerns." Abortion clinics and adoption agencies are also listed.

Local telephone directories have listings of state, county, and other agencies that can help pregnant teens. These include women's centers, WIC (Women, Infants, and Children) programs, the state department or bureau of Child Welfare, United Community Services, Catholic Charities, the Federation of Protestant Welfare Agencies, the United Federation of Jewish Philanthropies, and Women Organized Against Rape.

Other agencies that may be able to help you are listed below.

National Organizations

National Abortion Federation
1346 U Street NW
Washington, DC 20009
(202) 667-5881
(800) 772-9100
   The National Abortion Federation can tell you about the current abortion laws in your state and refer you to abortion services in your area.

National Adoption Information
   Clearinghouse
1400 Eye Street NW
Washington, DC 20005
(202) 842-1919
   The National Adoption Information Clearinghouse provides information on all aspects of adoption, including state and federal adoption

laws and the adoption of children with special needs. The organization also makes referrals to adoption agencies, crisis pregnancy centers, and support groups.

Planned Parenthood Federation
 of America
810 Seventh Avenue
New York, NY 10019
(212) 541-7800
Planned Parenthood provides information on birth control, disease prevention, and related topics. Local affiliates in most major cities operate clinics that offer confidential birth control education, pregnancy testing, gynecological exams, and other reproductive health services.

Hot Lines

A Call for Help (Canada)
(800) 537-2229

Herpes Resource Center Hotline
(919) 361-2120
Monday through Friday
9 a.m. to 6 p.m.

National AIDS Hotline
(800) 342-AIDS
24 hours, 7 days a week

National STD Hotline
(800) 227-8922
Monday through Friday
8 a.m. to 11 p.m.

Ottawa Rape Crisis Centre
 (Canada)
(613) 729-8889

Books for Young Adults

Bell, Ruth. *Changing Bodies, Changing Lives.* Vintage Books, 1988.

Bode, Janet. *Kids Still Having Kids.* Franklin Watts, 1992.

Brown, Fern G. *Teen Guide to Childbirth.* Franklin Watts, 1988.

DuPrau, Jeanne. *Adoption: The Facts, Feelings, and Issues of a Double Heritage.* Julian Messner, 1990.

Guernsey, JoAnn Bren. *Teen Pregnancy.* Clarion Books, 1989.

Lindsay, Jeanne Warren. *Open Adoption: A Caring Option.* Morning Glory Press, 1987.

McGuire, Paula. *It Won't Happen to Me.* Delacorte Press, 1983.

Nourse, Alan E. *Teen Guide to Safe Sex.* Franklin Watts, 1988.

Orr, Lisa. *Sexual Values.* Greenhaven, 1989.

Silverstein, Herma. *Teenage and Pregnant: What You Can Do.* Julian Messner, 1988.

Terkel, Susan Neiberg. *Abortion: Facing the Issues.* Franklin Watts, 1988.

Other Books on Teen Sexuality and Pregnancy

Calderone, Mary S., and Eric W. Johnson. *The Family Book About Sexuality.* Harper and Row, 1989.

Dash, Leon. *When Children Want Children: The Urban Crisis of Teenage Childbearing.* William Morrow, 1989.

Goldsmith, Sharon. *Human Sexuality: The Family Source Book.* C. V. Mosby Company, 1985.

Vecchiolla, Francine, and Penelope L. Maza. *Pregnant and Parenting Adolescents.* Children's Welfare League, 1989.

Zollar, Ann Creighton. *Adolescent Pregnancy and Parenthood: An Annotated Guide.* Garland, 1990.

INDEX